Copyright ©2016 by Kalilah C. Wright. All rights reserved.

This book or any portion thereof may not be reproduced or used in any manner whatsoever without the express written permission of the publisher except for the use of brief quotations in a book review. Printed in the United States of America & Thailand. First Printing, 2016 ISBN-13: 978-0692626139, ISBN-10: 0692626131

WWW.K-WRITE.COM

A Mother's Dream

Dedicated to my first born son, Kaiden Daniel Wright. Thank you for allowing me to embark on this journey of motherhood.

boy? girl?

Mommy always dreamt of having
the perfect little boy or girl.

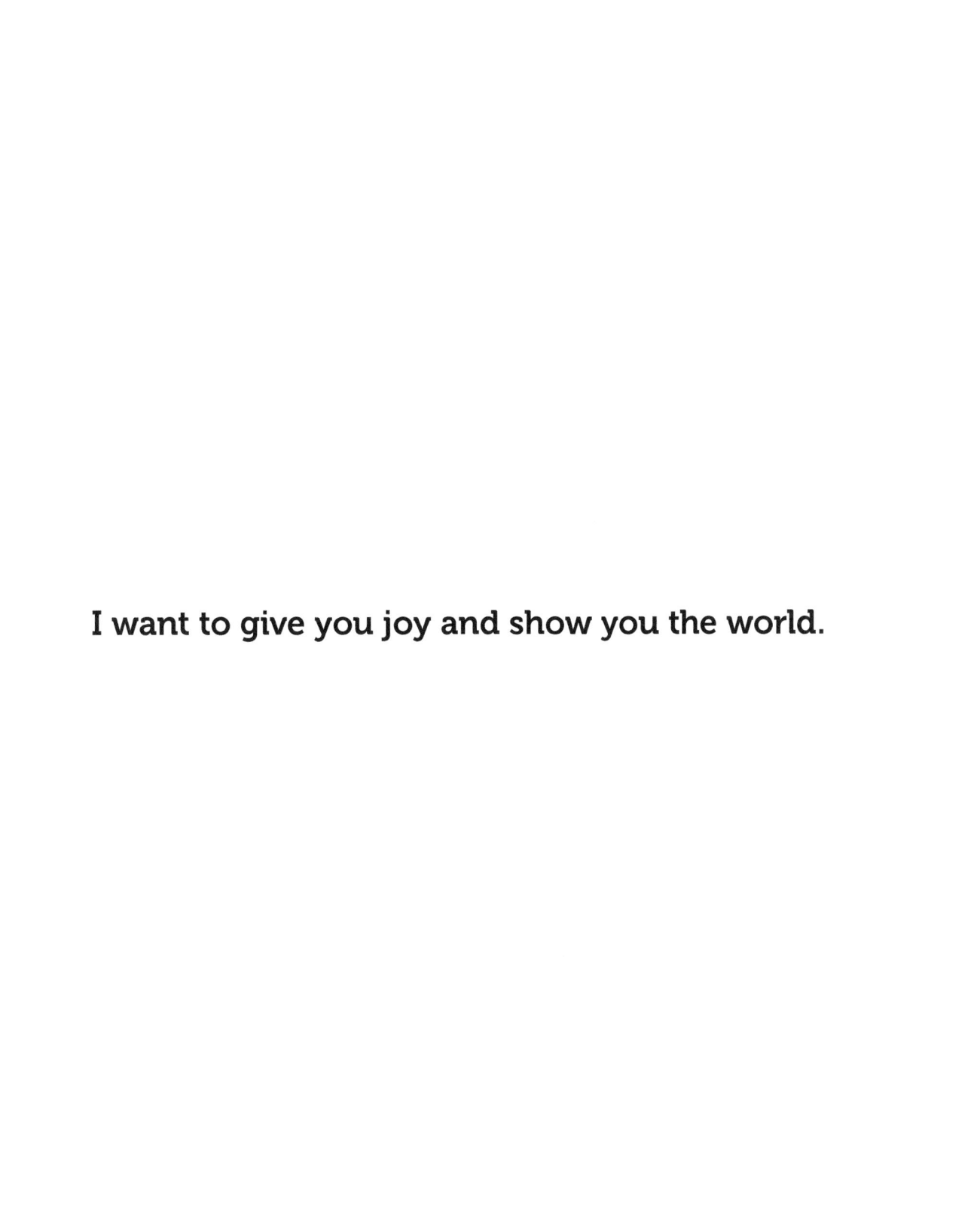

I want to give you joy and show you the world.

Mommy wants to kiss you at night.
I love you and want to see you smile bright.

Mommy wants to watch you take your first steps.

I never want to see you sad or upset.

Mommy wants to hold your hand tight.

I need to prepare you not to give up, but to fight.

Mommy wants to see you college-bound...

...standing proud and tall in your cap and gown.

Mommy can't wait to watch you walk down the aisle...

...to see you have your first baby, my loving grandchild.

These are the moments mommy has dreamt of and can't wait to see.

You are my treasure, my baby-to-be.

www.ingramcontent.com/pod-product-compliance
Lightning Source LLC
Chambersburg PA
CBHW060810090426
42736CB00003B/219